Pamala McCoy

A Community Shero's Story

Copyright © 2019 Sula Too Publishing. All rights reserved. This book may not be reproduced in whole or in part without written permission from the publisher, except by a reviewer who may quote brief passages in a review; nor may any part of this book be reproduced, stored in retrieval system, or transmitted in any form or by any means, electronic, mechanical, photocopying, recording, or other, without prior written permission from the copyright holder.

ISBN-13: 978-1-7339542-2-8 Paperback
Library of Congress Control Number:2019948793
ISBN-13: 978-1-7339542-3-5 eBook

Printed and bound in the United States of America September 2019

Published by
Sula Too Publishing
Tampa, Florida
www.sulatoo.com/publishing

Tiny Book Series - Book 1

Pamala McCoy

A Community Shero's Story

As told to Ersula K Odom

Recommended by Ralph Smith

Tiny Books by Sula Too Publishing
A division of Sula Too LLC
Tampa Florida

A Sula Too Publishing

Tiny Book Series

Sula Too Publishing Tiny Books offer stories of people and organizations spotlighting formative and celebrative moments that birth inspiration. Tiny Books give the reader a personal and professional peek into the subject's life, answering what, when and most often why.

The books have a similar look and feel, yet they are all very different. They offer comfort to those who see themselves in the stories and wisdom to those who find the stories unfamiliar.

Tiny Books are designed to give the subject a means of releasing top-of-mind information, that is on a loop in their heads, about those things they deem important or they are most proud. Your response to this Tiny Book may encourage an author to write a complete biography or inspire a autobiography where the rest of the story can be told.

Your story needs to be told and now is the time.

This book is a gift from

_____

This Shero's story
just may help someone find their purpose.

Introducing

Pamala McCoy

Our Community Hero
and
This is her Shero's Story

Contents

Introduction	12
Why - There Has to be A Reason	13
Purpose Evolution	15
What Does a 15 1/2-Year-Old Do With Money?	18
Parental Wisdom	20
Meet and Teach	29
I Thought I Knew What I Wanted	30
A Career Began to Develop	34
As Long as There is a Need	37

Pamala McCoy

Part I

Sula Too Tiny Book

Introduction

In this Tiny Book, Sula Too highlights the amazing story of Pamala McCoy and organizations she serves. Her story is destined to inspire entrepenuers, those with charitable hearts and those in need.

You, as the holder of this Tiny Book, have already been a blessing to someone.

May you also be motivated to tell your story. There are people who need to hear it.

Pamala McCoy

Why? - There Has to be A Reason

My most **profound memory** came during my freshmen year in college. After spending a wonderful Christmas break at home with my family in Goldsboro, North Carolina, I embarked on the one hour drive back to North Carolina State University in Raleigh, NC. Then, I was hit head on by a drunk driver, on a Sunday of all days.

Saying it was a profound moment is an understatement, but it was very pivotal for me.

I've always been a caring and passionate person concerned about other people. I relentlessly seek ways of giving back.

But in that moment, if you were to see my car, a Silver Toyota Corolla that I often explained, simply got me from point A to point B safely. Defending it, even though if anyone leaned on it they would probably put a dent in it.

At impact, it balled up like a piece of paper

and they had to use the Jaws of Life to get me out. A very traumatic, traumatic experience. Through it all, a lot of personal growth happened.

The most insightful thing was that with my being a faith based person, I knew in that moment that I truly had a purpose. In the journey of recovery, I fully understood that some people had been in accidents less impactful who did not survive. Anyone who saw my car had to wonder if anyone survived.

When I saw how crumbled my car was, I began an intense journey of discovering my purpose. Why was I saved? There had to be a reason.

The moment of impact was profound. I keep saying profound because I can't think of another word that is adequately descriptive of the feeling that this was a neccessary part of my journey towards discovering why I am here.

Pamala McCoy

Purpose Evolution

Compassion for people is my gift. Professionally, my background is in credit, credit cards, banking, and finance. I am most joyful when I'm conducting workshops, seminars, or one on one consultations. Providing people or groups information about how they can better themselves through improving their management decisions over their personal finances is valuable to me and to them. Finances are fundamental to everything that we do. When your money is not right, nothing is right.

During one of my seminars, I asked, "What was the correlation between your fiscal health and your physical health?" The attendees didn't know. People don't stop to think about that, but there is a direct correlation between your money and your body.

Whether you have a lot or a little, impacts are created by that fundamental foundational necessity for what we transact on called money. That's the driving force behind everything. Whether you have or have not, there are impacts because more money doesn't mean you have less stress. Ask millionaires and they'll tell you the more money, the more problems you could have.

Though not financial in the same regard as someone who's living in poverty, the stresses could very well be the same.

Surely, there was something else God wanted me to do, or it could have been lights out at the scene. However, I'm still here. This was not my earliest memory for I was 18 going on 19, in college, but truly a pivotal moment in my life.

I have always been fun, loving, and joyful. I've always been that optimist, the glass is half full kind of person and not wanting to dwell on the glass being half empty, even with regards to people that I knew. I started working when I was 15 and a half and as for the people that I work for and work with, it's always been my mindset that you can learn something from everyone ....even if it is what you don't want to be. So, we should be lifetime learners and every experience is a teachable moment. There's something to be learned from EVERYONE.

What Does a 15 & 1/2 Year-old Do With Money?

At fifteen and a half, I had to get a work permit which my parents had to approve and sign for. It was required by my very first real job, (other than babysitting), working at Hardee's Fast Food.

Similar to Tampa's Dale Mabry, Berkley was one of our main streets where countless fast food restaurants are up and down the street. As cheerleaders, we could be found working up and down the street because fast food places were the only businesses that would work around our schedule, and our afterschool extra-curricular activities.

So, every fast food establishment from Hardee's, McDonald's, Burger King, to pizza houses, we cheerleaders were all working on that street.

Cheerleading was all about team building, collaborating and working together as one. I cheered from junior high through high school.

Because of competitions we competed in, we quickly learned that cheering is not a "me" sport. To be great and to win, we had to work together. You can't have one superstar on the team for the team to be great.

These types of early lessons translates perfectly in what you do in corporate America or whatever job you hold. Teamwork truly does make the dream work. You can't be an I in a team and be as successful as you can be when you're working together collaboratively.

With that understanding, we had a great time. We played hard, we worked hard, but it was a lot of fun. A couple of the cheerleaders and I are still friends some 40 years later.

Working my first job was the onset, which now turns out to be my profession. It lead to my learning the financial responsibility that was required at home.

In our household, I was the youngest of four children. When I was fifteen, my older two brothers were already off at the United States Air Force Academy in Colorado. So it was just my sister and me at home.

My older sister and I are three years apart. My sister was working as well. Even though I was the youngest and my job was just a little part-time job, I still had to abide by the family rules about finances. My parents assigned both of us a bill to pay. Of course, things were not as costly then as they are now.

The second lowest bill was the cable bill, so that was my sister's responsibility to pay. I paid the newspaper lady.

I was set up with my own checking account and saving accounts. The rules were you pay your tithes, you pay yourself, you pay your bills. If there's nothing leftover, you sit at home and watch TV.

I first paid tithes on my little money that I was making, paid myself (i.e. my savings account, meaning paying into my future). And then, of course, my one little bill was the newspaper lady, which wasn't that much, but I had to be on time, write that check, and make sure she had it. Even though it wasn't a lot of money, it really wasn't about the money and my parents clearly saw that. It was about the lesson that you make a bill, you pay a bill. That's what you do. And you pay your bills on time.

I know life happens, but that was fundamental in my financial rearing. The irony is that what I am doing at Bona5d Credit Consultants is financial capability education. And those life lessons started so early on.

It is just entrenched in who I am.

Sula Too Tiny Book

Parental Talent and Wisdom

Dad: Dad went into the military and served 27 and a half years in the Air Force. He was security forces, which in the private sector, they were called the police. Therefore I had the opportunity to travel and live in many different places.

Being a military brat, as we're affectionately called, either you or your neighbor is moving approximately every three to five years. My lifestyle was vastly different from those who went to kindergarten and graduated with the same folks. I don't really know what that life would be like. I imagine there's a lot of benefits and things to being entrenched in the community. But that wasn't our lifestyle. Making up for a lack of community, I got to see parts of the world, experience different cultures, and different people.

Mom: My mother was an at-home mom part of the time, and she worked part of the time. My dad was old school and his philosophy and mindset was it is his job to provide for his family. He took that very seriously. And so, for my mom, it was work if you want to, if you don't want to, that's okay too.

Therefore, my mom worked periodically while we were growing up. When we were younger, she was at home keeping the home fires burning as they would say. Mom was a cosmetologist, and she was also gifted with crafting things. My mother could be walking in the mall, see someone with a suit on, go home, cut a pattern out of newspaper and wear the suit on Sunday.

She was gifted in that way with cooking, sewing, knitting, crocheting, embroidery, any and all of those crafty kind of things. It was just an innate ability for her, which might have come from her upbringing. There were 16 kids in my mom's family which included two sets of twins.

Making things and being creative was probably a necessity for them to stretch a dollar.

My mom made all of our Easter outfits. One year she made my prom dress, including the crinoline underneath. Another year she made my dress for the debutante ball. She could sew ANYTHING!

Even as an adult, when Mom came to visit she couldn't wait until I went to work. I kid you not... I left to go to work in the morning and when I got home at 5 o'clock, my mom had made a duvet cover, the pillow shams, and bedroom curtains. Yes. I was shocked, I was only gone for about eight hours. Really?

My parents being who they were personally and emotionally is what created my desire to always give. We were the house where kids would come, because Mom never met a stranger. You needed something to eat, **my mom's going to feed you**. We were that house where the kids hung out. There were only four biological kids in the home, but you look up at any given time, there might be eight or nine kids in the house because of all the neighbor kids, or someone spending the night.

That's just who my parents were, loving.

Education was always important. Growing up, for us kids, our number one job was to do well in school. I did not say to be an "A student" because they clearly recognized each one of us as individuals and that everyone may not have the capability to be an "A student," but we had to be our best. There's no room for mediocrity. That was driven home from day one. "You will always do your best, whatever that is." If your best is a B, then a C is not good enough. It's still passing, but it's not good enough because it wasn't your best.

We just had those foundational, fundamental things instilled in us, and it's organic. It wasn't like we sat down and said, "Okay, we're going to talk about education today or we're going to talk about money management today." They just lived and breathed it. Organically we got it.

We used to jokingly say that dad could squeeze the buffalo off a nickel. Again, the irony is that I now do what I do. Another lesson from my dad is - *he went into the United States Air Force and when he and my mom first got married, he had one stripe.*

Even when he wasn't making a lot of money, my dad could manage money like no one else. He put four kids through college. He did that. We were not millionaires or JD Rockefeller by any stretch of the imagination, but my dad was able to make it happen by making sound financial decisions.

Right. Dad could squeeze that buffalo right off the nickel.

When you put those two talented personalities together, you know what you have? You have Pamala.

Mother was a talented business woman. You can't run a cosmetology business and be a paid seamstress without being a businessperson. Even if you are working part time from home. People would hire her to do stuff because, like I said, "If she could see it, she could make it."

Mom was all around creative and a business creative as well as knew how to be disciplined and manage money. I am a by-product of all of that.

Pamala L. McCoy, Col. Victor E. Lofton (Ret.) brother, Rickey O. Lofton, Sr. brother, Angela J. Oxendine, sister

Pamala McCoy

Meet and Teach

A friend of mine once said, which is so true, **I am a part of all whom I have met.** I thought that was profound. I believe you can learn something from everybody, even if it's a negative, you learn something that you don't want to do. When you receive that and implement it in your life, then that person did pour something positive into your life and was useful to you.

I Thought I Knew What I Wanted

I'm a graduate from North Carolina State University in Raleigh, NC, with a degree in business management with a concentration in economics. When I first went to college, I considered a computer science major. I was intrigued by robotics and at that time, there weren't very many women in robotics, and needless to say, nor many African American women in robotics. I was seeing the dollar signs. I was going to be great. This was going to be the journey.

I started out in Computer Science. After a couple of nights at the lab trying to write code and stuff, and I was like, oh, hey, hey, hey, this is not for me. Clearly you understand you need to pay your dues before you get into the promise land kind of thing, but I just know I can't do coding, that it doesn't light my fire. Then, I thought, well, I've always been into fashion and one day I want to own a boutique and all that is retail. But the more I learned about the time, effort and energy it takes, every holiday, all of that, you're there and away from your family, that then came off my bucket list because family is really important to me.

Then, I like numbers, so I thought, well, maybe accounting, but I'd never even signed up for accounting in terms of a degree because though I like numbers, I have to have people engagement. And so, credit became that blend, that mix of I have numbers, but I'm touching people. That's how my career path started. A few false starts and thinking, I want to do this and changing your mind. And so, for those listeners who are young, it's okay. You're writing it in pencil for a reason because you can erase and change your mind. We don't have to use ink pens when we're doing this planning called life kind of thing. So, doing what I did career-wise and even what I do today in my consulting company, it allows me the best of both worlds because I can't be behind the desk, or like an accountant with the what they call the pocket protector and all of that. I got to have people engagement, the conversation. I have to impact lives.

I have to have conversation and pour into people. That's really important to me. Again, when they're talking about finding your purpose, your purpose is something, when people ask me, I say we all need money because we have to pay our bills and that's how we transact in this thing we call life. If money wasn't a driver and wasn't relevant at all, what's the one thing that you would do for free? That thing you can't let go. Even if you wanted to try and do something else, yeah, you might be kind of happy, but you're not ecstatic. But that thing, whatever that is for you, then that is your purpose and because purpose chooses you, you don't choose the purpose. If that makes sense.

So much goes back to your upbringing, and your upbringing is not only your home, but your environment. Some of it is genetics, but environment plays a role in that. All change is not bad just like all change is not good. We can't throw away the baby with the bath water kind of thing. Some of the things that they did old school, would be beneficial today. As parents or leaders of our community, I think that it's our responsibility to incorporate some of those old things into the new things to move us forward.

A Career Began to Develop.

The bulk of my career has been in collections... even I thought when I was in the training program, oh no ... We used to call it escaping the collection clutches. No one wanted their assignment to be in collections. But once I got in collections, how about I never looked back. Because it gives you an opportunity to educate people. It gives you an opportunity to provide hope for people and to look at people beyond their circumstances. Because in collections, everyone who is delinquent and in collections is not defined as a dead beat. Life happens, and it depends on how prepared you are, for when it happens, how well you move through that journey or what-have-you. So, being able to problem solve and help folks problem solve and see beyond this circumstance and provide that hope in spite of their circumstance was probably a life lesson for me and a driver for me and helped me define my purpose.

No one thought I wanted to be in collections,

but collections really was for me, a ministry. It gave me an opportunity **to teach, to share, to provide hope, to share my faith** when appropriate and really just to empower people. So, the motto of my company now is "educate, empower, evolve, enlighten, enrich." Those five Es are the foundation of what we do and pouring into people. And as far as giving back, beyond what I do professionally, outreach has always been a part of who I am. And as I've gotten grown and moving forward, I do believe to whom much is given, much is required and giving back is just innately a part of who I am. So, I do outreach from feeding the homeless, clothing the homeless, providing some pro bono work in terms of what I do professionally.

Sula Too Tiny Book

Part II

Pamala McCoy

As Long as There is a Need

Maurice D. McCoy, Sr. (CMSgt – Ret) husband / Pamala L. McCoy

My husband and I have a group of folks that we call our **Keep Tampa Warm Team,** on our quest to keep people warm. Even though we only go out two or three times a year (remember it is Florida) to distribute blankets and warm clothes, my outreach is year round.

In order to provide clothing, I partner with some organizations, some consignment shops and some nonprofits. Therefore I have clothing on a regular basis, so much so we've converted one of our guest rooms into **"The McCoy Distribution Center."** During the year when I'm getting clothing donations, we're passing them out all year. I pull out all of the winterish items, such as hoodies, sweaters, and any heavier items. We put them off to the side.

When the temperature drops below 40 degrees here in Tampa, which only happens a few times a year, we activate the Keep Tampa Warm Team. I have a partnership with a couple of McDonald's whose owners provide coffee and condiments to me. I also have a source that provide blankets. So, we give out blankets, coffee and items from all the warm clothing that I've accumulated.

With money that is donated, we buy socks. The socks are used for feet and for hands during these winter months. We don't buy gloves in Florida because they are not readily available.

We move out, literally like a convoy in route to where the homeless are, and pop the trunk. We provide. We serve. If you ever have the opportunity, I tell you, it is life changing.

There's not been one time we haven't been on this mission when something reflective didn't happen or was said. For example, the very first time we provided blankets and clothes, but I didn't have coffee. It really hadn't even dawned on me to do so. Or like when we pulled up and a gentleman approached us and said, "I just said to my wife, it's going to be so cold tonight, I don't know what we're going to do. Then you guys pulled up with blankets." That was moving. That was a moment. We could have been at a stop light and missed seeing him. Why did we show up right after he made that statement? "God Is So Crazy Cool"(TM). He orchestrated that encounter. When you have faith the size of a mustard seed, you ask, and He provides. Just like that.

That was a faith moment for that gentleman.

Sula Too Tiny Book

I don't know where he is spiritually, but now he's got to believe something that he spoke into the universe and voila, a blanket appeared.

During that faithful first day, another God moment came in the form of a question. Someone asked, do you happen to have something hot to drink? We didn't, but that planted a seed. It was a Wednesday and it was predicted that it was going to be cold again that Friday. I was determined to solve this problem by then. I got a five gallon container, and I set out to have something hot for the people to drink. It's no joke when I say that God comes through every time I call. I stopped at the McDonald's down the street from my church and the person I needed to talk to someone who wasn't there. We didn't connect at all that day.

Thursday, about 6 o'clock she called back, and told me she'd put in a call to the owner of the McDonald's. She needed approval because I asked for five gallons, not just a pot of coffee. And less than 30 minutes later, he had called her back and said, "Certainly just drop off the container, we'll have it full with the coffee, all the condiments, and everything you need. If we had known sooner, we could have sent hamburgers."

It just was amazing, there was three McDonald's within less than a five mile radius, and he owned two of them. His brother-in-law owned the other one. So, whenever I need coffee, all I need to do is pick up the phone, and they come through for me every single time that we provide that liquid gold.

Because when the folks on the street have a cup of hot coffee, and the temperatures are dropping, it's a blessing.

However, this is not something you can do alone. It takes people stepping outside of themselves. You don't ever have to have been homeless to be empathetic and to understand what it would be like. We need to each ask ourselves the what if, because there but for the grace of God, go I. Tomorrow's a new day. You've got a roof over your head, but if you take time to talk to some of these folks, they were just like us. They had homes, they had cars, they had jobs, they had clothes, all that, but then life happened.

Now, we each need to just step outside of ourselves and consider, "If that was me on the other side, how would I want people to treat and respond to me?" Well, if you're honest, you would want people to look beyond your circumstance and see you. Thus, that's how I approach what I do in terms of giving back. I have been blessed so many ways. I'm not a Rockefeller, don't have $1 million, but what I have is a blessing that wasn't intended for me. He blesses us to be a blessing to someone else. So, it's important to me to give back.

Our church sends a van to Salvation Army every Sunday to bring anyone to church who wants to come. We, the church's **Salvation Army Outreach Team**, provide them breakfast. Of course, then **I provide them clothing if needed.** They go to the service. We provide lunch before we take them back. That's every Sunday, all year round. We do that in partnership with the Salvation Army.

I am a **mentor for USF School of Business** and have been for the past **10 years.** I've had about 10 mentees, formally assigned plus additional informal ones, who were first generation college students. They didn't really have that roadmap from home on what to do. The mentorship program was established for that reason, just to teach and show them some things that they were not going to get in a textbook.

I partner with **Dress For Success.** I provide services for them in several areas. Financial literacy, administrative tasks and I help them teach basic Microsoft skills. They're teaching women who want to reenter the workforce. They all have a story. Some as simple as they took time off to raise their children and now they want to return to work. Some of them have had brushes with law enforcement, incarceration or even domestic violence. Whatever the story, I partner with Dress For Success to facilitate their efforts.

I partner with **Pace**, which is an alternative school for young at risk girls. Again, just trying to give them another path, another way of looking at life.

When I'm working with youth I like to say, "Exposure levels the playing field." What I mean by that is these at risk kids often times have not been beyond their own neighborhoods. We help them to know the possibilities are endless and that their possibilities are only limited because they haven't had the exposure.

Being in a position to expose young people to college or behind the scenes business tours is wonderful. I've been blessed with television appearances where **I give "bona5d bits"** on various networks. My relationships at the networks allow me to take my teens **behind**

the scenes to see what goes on at a news station where they can spend the day and be a shadow.

If they never see what an anchor person, or camera person, or the producer does, then how can they even aspire to do what they never even knew existed? I enjoy pouring into youth.

The summer of 2019 was my seventh year conducting **F.I.T. Camp (Financially Intelligent Teens) with Solita's House**, a nonprofit. We are taking typically 13 to 17-year-olds from a lower economic band, and teaching them basic fundamentals of personal money management. The camp usually takes place the last two weeks of July. They can go to the website to sign up on the website and we take 20 students on a first come first serve basis. It's an excellent nonprofit camp based on fundamentally sound principles. So much so, one year I flew my niece in from North Carolina to attend the camp. It's powerful. It's a necessity.

I volunteer during **Great American Teach-In** every year in several schools. I've worked with the **Boys and Girls Club** and the **Black Business Bus Tour**. I just try to stay engaged.

Powernet, which is a nonprofit that's dealing with reentry. Putting together programming for people who had been incarcerated but now are needing to reenter society, making sure that they are connected with resources that are available to them.

I'm a part of the **Hillsborough county Parenting Resource Coalition**, getting children resources that they need, but looking at it from a holistic approach in that the family has to be informed for the children to benefit.

Magnificent Me$^{(TM)}$. They target young girls eight to twelve years old. That's a Christian base camp that takes place during the summer.

I partner with **Computer Mentors**. They conduct an annual teen business challenge. That's an awesome, awesome opportunity for youth. They learn leadership and presentation skills. They learn team building, team work and collaboration. They learn how to pitch an idea. They learn how to write a business plan, to spark that entrepreneurial spirit in our children. Gone are the days where we need to just plan to go work for a company for 30 years, get a gold watch, and retire. That path isn't necessarily the path for everyone. Our kids, if they're not exposed to entrepreneurship, how do they know about entrepreneurship? That levels the playing field and opens all kinds of doors to finding their purpose. When you're walking in your purpose, it doesn't feel like work. Is this something that you enjoy doing, and you happen to get paid for it? That's very, very important.

I work with some **women's groups**, women in wealth, again related to finance, and some work with **Youth Build,** which is a nonprofit that falls under the **Tampa Housing Authority.**

Most of the youth haven't made it in traditional school, needed to get their GEDs, and find a path for themselves. That path is not necessarily college, it may be learning a trade. During FIT camp, we don't always say going to college, we like to refer to it as "your next", because your next is not college for everybody. Next could be going to trade school such as truck driving or cosmetology school.

Blanket Tampa Bay founded by Beth Ross meets every Monday, rain or shine, hell or high water, at St. Peter Claver Church handing out food and clothing and toiletries. So, if anyone wants to volunteer, they don't need to sign up, just show up. We'll put all hands to work. When you have a heart for serving people, the opportunities just come but unfortunately, what do they say? The harvest is plenty of the workers are few or something like that. So, you just got to make yourself available to impact people. I honestly believe that it is reciprocal.

A nonprofit that is near and dear to my heart

is **Shalon's Hope** founded by Shalon Barnett. The goal is to build a home or acquire other properties, to provide transitional housing and affordable transitional housing for women. Affordable housing in the Tampa Bay area is really nonexistent for the most part. These ladies came from **DACCO,** are conquering their demons and they're wanting to turn their life around. If not for Shalon's Hope, that would be much more difficult for them. The housing they could potentially afford is not in an environment that they need to be in, considering their demons. So, that's a nonprofit too that's near and dear to my heart to be able to provide financial literacy, support, hope and just really being there to support the women.

I partnered with the **BEST Program** and BEST stands for the Brain Expansion Scholastic Training. They target high school and college students driven in the medical field. Again, it's exposing these kids to these opportunities that they don't even know exists. When you think of the medical field, on the surface, it might be very limited. I go to the doctor, so there's a doctor, well, I don't want to be a doctor. But medical field is much deeper than that, young people need to know this.

I worked with the **RENEW Group.** They took some "at risk kids" to NASA. When I say exposure, these kids, when they think NASA, they think going to the moon and that's all there is, and they respond with "I'm not leaving the earth." But NASA is exponentially much deeper than that. In the movie Hidden Figures, that was about math. Those ladies never left the earth, but they were able to share their knowledge. There are so many disciplines the kids are most likely not aware of.

Pamala McCoy

Positioning to Be Able to Give

I've been blessed. My husband served 30 years in the military and his MOS(military occupational specialty) was finance and my profession is also in finance. Again, I cannot stress it enough that personal money management is fundamental in everyone's life. I don't care if you got $5, $50, or $5 million, it's really not about the zeroes. It's about the decisions that you make with the money that you have. It's not about how much money you make, it's about how much money you keep. It also helps that my husband is a God fearing man who believes in outreach and giving of time, talent, and treasure.

It works itself out when you're walking in your purpose. You don't really know how it works. You just know that it's working, and it's working because He's allowing it to work. I can be up all night long preparing to present. When I'm on the stage, I'm on. I can sleep later. I give my 110% every single time that I'm on.

Sula Too Tiny Book

A couple of years ago we wanted to do something special for the ladies at the Salvation Army for Christmas, some **girly stuff.** A group of us got together for this mission and instead of gift bags, we used **reusable bags for Christmas gift bags**. When you're thinking about homelessness, you have put yourself in their place. They need something that they can reuse, they need something that they can carry around, etc.

People gave us donations that we used to buy bras and panties, because we really wanted this to be a girly, girly thing. The amount of items received was like a freight arriving. Additionally, I purchased a couple of pallets of various kinds of makeup including lipstick, lip gloss and eyeliner from Feeding America. All things girly. It was exciting knowing how much joy we were going to deliver.

I went to the flea market and was pulling all kinds of different sizes and styles of bras and panties which caught the attention of the store owner. She walks over to me because what I was doing was weird. Usually people go in to get their own size. She asked, "What are you doing?" I shared with her who I was shopping for... and how about she then donated. People really do want to help. So, she did, she added to my pile of things that I was buying.

We went to the Salvation Army and we preloaded the bags with the basic stuff, toiletries, soaps and lotions. We formed an assembly line for the ladies to move through and pick out the makeup, because you can't preload makeup. They could chose face powder or lipstick or gloss or eyeliner based on skin tone and texture.

At the end of the line, they could pick out a bra and a pair of panties. We just take so many things for granted. Once a lady asked, "Can I have a red one? I've always wanted a red one.". Just little things, little things like that can mean so much. To be able to gift someone that feeling is beyond what words can describe.

Sula Too Tiny Book

During one trip to the Salvation Army when we were feeding people, a young guy ran over to us, with a key on a chain around his neck, and said, "I just had to tell you guys, this is the key to my very first apartment, and I'm moving in tomorrow." I cried because I know I would never look at a house key the same again. When you walk into your house, you throw your keys on the table. They're just keys. They don't have that kind of meaning. What I thought about the key around his neck is, he had on pants with pockets; he had on a shirt with a pocket. His actions said, "I'm afraid to put it in my pocket because I'll lose it, so I want it close to my heart because this is the first key to my first place.

I remember my first apartment, it didn't feel that way because I'd never been homeless. And so, If you went from this house to that house ... it was just the key. But for him, it was a key. I just thought I'll never look at a house key the same way.

Pamala McCoy

It's Not A Matter of Money

It's not even a matter of the money. Oftentimes, your time or your talent is what's needed. People don't give equally because we're not equally yoked financially.

In the Bible, they told the story of the lady who just gave her little money, her one cent, where everybody was giving dollars and dollars, and this is in modern times, so not in the biblical time. Most people gave dollars and she gave a penny. But the difference was the penny was her last. That doesn't have the same value as when you're giving from your lack. I don't have much, but I gave.

When people are giving, maybe you don't have the money to give, but how about you take some time to volunteer somewhere. Maybe you are very talented at X, Y, Z, and that talent is needed in this organization. So, how about donating your talent. Whether it's baking, it's sewing, basket weaving, repairing things, whatever. You may not have the money to give, but you can give your talent, you can give your time. That is as valuable as money, and I would venture to say in a lot of cases, more valuable than the money.

Just like when you hear successfully raised children say, "We grew up in poverty, we were poor, but we were very rich." What does that mean? They didn't have a lot of money, but the house was full of love. They didn't realize they were poor until they were adults.

What is it really all about? Just looking beyond yourself on behalf of someone else. That doesn't take money. No, that doesn't take money, it just takes the right heart.

Pamala McCoy

Pamala McCoy

For the Good of the Community

According to your contact:*

_____

_____

_____

A portion of the proceeds from the sale of this book will benefit the following organization:

_____

_____

_____

*If the sale of this book is being used for fundraising, the person named here is solely responsible for ensuring the proceeds are delivered to the designated recipient

Sula Too Tiny Book

Sponsor:

Ralph Smith Founder and CEO of Computer Mentors Group, Inc which prepares Hillsborough County students for careers in computers and technology.

Founded in 1977 by Ralph Smith. In 2014 CMG began providing computers to newly housed veterans. www.computermentors.org.

Publisher:

Ersula K Odom – Sula Too Publishing

Author, historian and publisher. Creator of the Tiny Book Series.

Nominations for future books can be submitted at www.sulatoo.com/tinybooks

Pamala McCoy

Ms. Pamala L. McCoy graduated in 1989 with a BA-Business Management with a concentration in Economics from North Carolina State University (NCSU). She went on to hold various progressing positions in two private label credit entities: Sears Credit and Service Merchandise headquarters and moved to Tampa in 1998.

At that time, Pamala joined the then recently charted, TCM Bank, N.A. responsible for setting things up for all things credit, such as, policies and procedures for New Account, Customer Service, Collections, Fraud,

Probate and everything in between.

Pamala is currently CEO of BONA5D Credit Consultants, LLC and is a board member of the Tampa Mayor's African American Advisory Council (since 2015), where she served as the Economic Stability Chair; advisory board member for The Renew Group (since 2013); advisory board member for PowerNet (2017); mentor for USF Muma School of Business (since 2010); serves on the membership committee of the Regional Black Chamber of Commerce (since 2017); as well as active in numerous other community volunteerism opportunities.

On a personal note, Pamala married the love of her life, Maurice D. McCoy, Sr. in 1995. He proudly served 30 years in the United States Air Force, retiring at the highest enlisted rank of Chief Master Sergeant. They are the proud parents of four boys and eight grandchildren. When asked about her hobbies, her response was "volunteering to serve others is my hobby."

Pamala is passionately inspired by her faith, her family, her work, her volunteerism … and her goal is to strengthen her community by each individual she is blessed to impact.

Pamala McCoy

ALSO BY PAMALA MCCOY

Bona5d Bits: Where Inspiration & Intellect Collide With Your Finances
www.BONA5DCC.com

ALSO BY ERSULA K ODOM

At Sula's Feet

Doris Ross Reddick

African Americans of Tampa

www.ingramcontent.com/pod-product-compliance
Lightning Source LLC
Chambersburg PA
CBHW052118070526
44584CB00017B/2543